NATIVE KNOWINGS

WISDOM KEYS FOR ONE AND ALL

A COMPILATION BY
STEVEN MCFADDEN

2008 - updated 2023
ISBN: 978-1-7923-0927-4

Soul*Sparks Books
An imprint of Light and Sound Press, LLC
Tiwa Territory, Albuquerque, New Mexico, U.S.A.
lightandsoundpress.com

LICENSE NOTES

Acknowledgements

A great many people have earned my appreciation and my thanks for their influence and help. All honored. Thank you also to the talented photographers of pixabay.com. I thank in particular my Muse and partner in life, Elizabeth Wolf.

I thank also fellow pilgrim Bill Watkinson who helped me get my feet on the trail many years ago, and all of the many learned elders it has been my good fortune to encounter. Great thanks also to the elders of eras past, whose enduring messages are woven into this small treasure, entwined in chorus with the voices of contemporary elders that they all may be remembered.

Tobacco and honor songs for all, I offer in respect and appreciation. — S.M.

Introduction

It has been my work in life to write about the Earth through reporting on farms and farmers, conversing with many pioneers of clean, uplifting agriculture, and also to visit with indigenous spiritual elders, paying respectful attention. I've listened with care to try to understand the teachings they all have offered about the Earth and about the era of transition in which we live. *Native Knowings* is part of my efforts as an independent journalist to pass along some of those understandings.

This modest Soul*Sparks volume cannot hope to encompass the many levels and depths of understanding that are part of indigenous traditions. But it can point toward them, and it can do so in a manner appropriate for our raucous era. Some things—core spiritual truths such as honesty, caring, sharing, respect, and beauty—remain constant as a focus for our aspirations through all phases and cycles of human and world development. Eternal virtues. Those virtues lie at the heart of these native knowings.

My aim as compiler has been to offer in context what has touched me as a quintessence of both ancient and contemporary native knowings in a coherent, and rhetorically strengthening manner. The state of the world, in my view, calls for the very best we human beings can enact. Thus I feel called to share what I can comprehend, and to make it readily and reasonably accessible as we confront mounting environmental and social crises in North America and around the world.

Indisputably, big changes are underway. My hope is that this small volume will in some ways help human beings move through the changes more wisely. The root teachings of North America—native knowings—can truly help. This I know in the core of my being.

As we confront the complex problems of national cultures and ecosystems in radical transition, most people are looking for ways forward. While striving forward, we would do well to consider thoughtfully the voices that arise from Earth-based cultures, and to weave their enduring insights—developed on this land over millennia—into the fabric of what we are creating for ourselves, for our children, and for our children's children.

Native peoples and cultures are as diverse as any other human community. There is no one point of view. The passages assembled in *Native Knowings* are but a sample, and in no way represent any official or comprehensive expression of native views. They are simply knowings that have been of value to me, and that I feel can likewise be of value for others.

Still, the indigenous peoples of the Americas generally hold in common traditions of democracy and also wholesome pathways of spiritual development, pathways that have been tried and tested over many thousands of years. Speaking broadly, as elders have often reminded me, native peoples generally agree that they hold a specific spiritual responsibility as keepers of the Earth. This understanding provides ground for appreciating the compelling relevance of indigenous wisdom in a time of rapid evolution.

As Algonquin Grandfather William Commanda said while we were on the road together back in 1995, "We cannot order or demand anyone to do anything. We can only tell you what we know and hope and pray that you will listen. We native people know something. After having lived here on this land for many thousands of years, we have learned some things. We don't know it all, but we do know something.

"Right now we all have a choice, but that choice is very hard," Grandfather said. "But we must make that choice now so that our children will have the possibility of the life that we have had. We love you. We love you all, and we are depending on you to help us make life possible for our children and for your children."

Some of the passages in this slender volume are drawn from a presentation made by 28 traditional Native American elders, including Grandfather Commanda, at the "House of Mica," United Nations headquarters in New York City, on November 22, 1993 at the historic *Cry of the Earth* conference.

Sponsored by the Crescentera Foundation, *Cry of the Earth* was an unprecedented gathering of world leaders with traditional elders from North America, intended to focus attention on the ecological, economic, ethical, and spiritual crises confronting humanity.

Nary a word of the elders' remarkable messages was reported at the time by mass media. Despite notice, news businesses turned their backs to the elders and to their eloquent, insightful messages, thereby depriving the public of opportunities to hear and understand. *Native Knowings* endeavors to compensate in some assistive way for that gross oversight.

It is my passionate understanding that people have a right to hear and to contemplate the words of the elders. It's also my understanding that their individual and collective insight can make a positive and important difference. That's one reason for this compilation.

While a handful of passages in this book are drawn from messages publicly delivered at *Cry of the Earth*, and others are drawn from historical and literary sources, substantial passages come from my notes. As a journalist it has been a key part of my work to seek out and to converse with human beings wise in the ways of earth and spirit. I've woven some of what I have been privileged to hear into these pages.

I've no high commission, validating agency, tribal group, or foundation supporting, or influencing my work. I am, as all must be, an imperfect messenger. Yet having recognized what I regard as vital messages, my soul compels me to echo them as truly and respectfully as I am able.

As Grandfather William Commanda related many times when discussing the set of teachings known as the Seven Fires of the Anishinaabe, each "fire" can be understood to symbolize an era of time. During the time of the Seventh Fire, widely regarded as our era, it was said that "new people" will emerge. They will have opportunities to learn, to cooperate, and to move life forward in positive ways.

I choose to stand among these pioneers, intending with them to weave the tested and true wisdom knowings of the land with the brilliance of the high-tech ways emerging so dynamically, yet so often with heedless regard for the next seven generations of our children. That's of central consequence at this moment of our development. May it be that science and spirit respectfully entwine for the good of everyone and everything in the Sacred Hoop of life.

As one person with caring and curiosity, I've had opportunities to ask learned elders from many traditions for understanding and guidance, as have indeed many other people. For these opportunities I'm deeply grateful.

The passages and quotations in this book call upon us not to imitate or to try in some false or awkward way to become native peoples, but rather simply to listen, to respect the circle of life of which we are part, to be ourselves, and to endeavor to become the best human beings we possibly can.

The words of contemporary leaders in particular are tinged with a note of urgency. They share a sense that the time for us to make profound changes in our attitudes and our behaviors is short. They encourage us to consider their voiced offerings promptly and carefully. — S.M.

THEY WILL RETURN MY FRIEND

They will return my friend,
They will return again.
All over the Earth,
They are returning again.

Ancient teachings of the Earth,
Ancient songs of the Earth.
They are returning

I give them to you,
And through them
You will understand.
You will see.

They are returning again
Upon the Earth.

— THASÚNKE WITKÓ, CRAZY HORSE, OGLALA LAKOTA

Time of the Seventh Fire

"The Seventh Prophet who long ago spoke to the people was different from the others. He was young, and he had a distinct light in his eye. When he spoke, he said 'In the time of the Seventh Fire new people will emerge. They will retrace their steps to find what was long ago left by the side of the trail. Their steps will take them to the elders, who they will ask to guide them on their journey. But many of the elders will have fallen asleep. They will awaken to this new time with little to offer. Some of the elders will be silent out of fear, having seen their people persecuted for their ways. But most of the elders will be silent because no one will ask anything of them."

— Ojshigkwanàng (William Commanda), Traditional Chief, Kitigan Zibi Anishinaabe, holder of the Seven Fires Wampum Belt for many decades. He often shared teachings from Bawdwaywidun (Eddie Benton-Banai), and other Anishinaabe tradition holders

The Eastern Door

"Just this year (1993) the opening of the Eastern Door took place in Cape Spear, Newfoundland, Canada, the furthest eastern point in North America. The circle of the Medicine Wheel is now complete.

"The Wabanaki (People of the Morning Light) have joined the circle under the following philosophy: 'Heal you the self. You help to heal the family, the family helps to heal the community, the community helps to heal the nation, the nation helps to heal the world.

"It is time for all of us to stop blaming one another, heal from our wounds, and move forward, for the survival of our world as we know it is in our hands."

— DAVID GEHUE, MI'KMAQ, AT *CRY OF THE EARTH*

The Fire Burning

"According to the teachings of our native elders, and according to the teachings that have come through the Ywahoo lineage, the Earth will not be destroyed by man's armaments and munitions. If the Earth should decide to shake people free, it would be the fire burning—the fire that comes to purify the aggressive tendencies of mind."

— VEN. DHYANI YWAHOO, TSALAGI (CHEROKEE)

WHERE WE'RE HEADED

"If we don't change our direction,
we're likely to end up where we're headed."

— RUBEN SNAKE, HO-CHUNK (WINNEBAGO), EARTH DAY 1993

SPEAK ONLY TRUTH

"Our fathers gave us many laws, which they had learned
from their fathers. These laws were good. They told us to
treat all people as they treated us, that we should not be
the first to break a bargain, that it was a disgrace to tell a
lie, that we should speak only the truth. We were taught
to believe that the Great Spirit sees and hears everything,
and that he never forgets; that hereafter he will give every
man a spirit-home according to his deserts…"

— CHIEF JOSEPH, NEZ PERCE

Big Changes Are Coming

"Big changes are coming in this frame of time. All the elders know that. That's why it's important to talk now and tell people to respect Mother Earth, and to stop destroying the water, air, and mountains. We must respect all the creations of the Creator, and stop making those kinds of technologies that affect the solar rays that come to us on Earth. True scientists must think of our children. Care for each other. Love each other without discrimination. That is my main message.

"We are in times of big changes for the Earth, big earthquakes and hurricanes, also big conflicts in politics and war. They (politicians) promise changes. But we know that at their big meetings, done in the name of making things better, they do not make changes that work. It's the same old thing. The people must make the changes themselves."

— **Don Alejandro Cirilo Perez Oxlaj, Daykeeper, Maya**

House of Mica
United Nations Headquarters
Manhattan

WE INHERIT A SACRED RESPONSIBILITY

"A great prophecy had foretold the arrival of relatives of the many colors…Our sacred, unfulfilled destiny today rises to fulfillment in native and pilgrim descendants and all peoples.

"The great prophesy lives powerfully in the tapestry of America's diverse natives and diverse peoples, religions, cultures, and languages…Now we inherit the sacred responsibility to renew and complete the spiritual-political culture on this land, and around this world. We do so by reconciling the past, and healing the present."

— CHIEF SONNE REYNA, YAQUI-CARRIZO NATIONS

YOU MUST FIGURE IT OUT

"Don't look to us for your answers. Our way is not *The Way*. Look into your own heart, and come as close to the voice of your own heart as you can so you can hear the voice of your own heritage. You must figure it out, and see through which tradition it will speak. You must find your own way."

— MANUEL HOYONGOWA, HOPI, AT *CRY OF THE EARTH*

THIS IS THE HOLY LAND

"I'm always a little surprised when I hear people say that they are getting on a plane and heading off to the Holy Land. Because the Holy Land is here. This is it right here in America. We are standing right now on Holy Land. My people have known that forever, and it's time everyone came to understand it."

— WINONA LADUKE, OJIBWE, AT CHIEF STANDING BEAR HONOR BREAKFAST, LINCOLN, NEBRASKA, MAY 2010

THE GREAT MESSAGE

"We have only one Creator, all of us. We have many ways of understanding or speaking about this, but only one Creator…

"…We have to walk softly. That's it. Native people have, in these times, been called by Great Mystery to come forward, and that's what we are doing: at the United Nations, in Ottawa, in Washington, and in Mexico City.

"We are giving the Great Message that we have carried all these many thousands of years. We are giving the Great Message of our indigenous nations because we love you, and we care about you, and we want to help you. Help us, and we will help you.

"In the spiritual way of life there is no room for hate, no room for jealousy, no room for greed. You must have love in your heart, and you must have patience; then you can follow the spiritual way. This is what we know. This is what we say.

"A long time ago, at the time of creation, Creator created people of different colors and gave them their instructions. From these different colors came all the people. As we have been told by our grandmothers and grandfathers, our people, the Red people, were the last to get their instructions. We were told: 'Take care of this Mother Earth.' This is the instruction that was given. Also, we were told: 'Take care of these people of the other colors, and everything that Creator created. Take care.'

"This was repeated four times, to make sure that it was understood and acknowledged, and I am acknowledging it again today...

"...This is the last thing we have to share with you. The land, it is gone. We have shared how we fish, we have shared how we trap, we have shared how we grow corn, and beans, and squash. This is the last thing we have, our spiritual way. And now it is coming out, because it is very important that we give it to you now. We give it to you because it is very important, and because we love you. These are the teachings of our hearts.

"I ask you to listen not just with your minds. I ask you to listen with your hearts. Because that is the only way you can receive what it is, what we are giving. These are the teachings of our hearts.

"We Native people see what is going on. We see the fish are gone. We see that there are no cod any longer here on Cape Cod. We see the trees are dying. We see that the fresh waters are now bitter. We see the people suffering everywhere. We see the animals dying. We see the hole in the sky. We don't need to go into a laboratory to understand this. We see it with our eyes, and with our hearts. We see what is going on.

"We want to live. We want to survive. We want our children to live, and to be part of the Sacred Hoop...Be patient. Listen to the elders. You need patience to receive these teachings. It doesn't all come at once. You need patience."

— FRANK DECONTIE, KITIGAN ZIBI ANISHANABEG, ORATION AT FIRST ENCOUNTER BEACH, MASSACHUSETTS, JUNE 23, 1995

MANITOU

"The world of the Native American, spiritual and otherwise, is not to be understood by assuming that it can be described easily in the English language, and in religious terms. What we now think of as spirituality was not a religion in the commonly accepted definition of the word. It was their way of life, which is to say it permeated their lives to such an extent as to be inseparable from everyday living...Manitou was not a supreme being but rather a way of referring to the cosmic, mysterious power existing everywhere in nature."

— EUNICE BAUMANN-NELSON, PH.D., PENOBSCOT

WHAT IS LIFE?

"What is life? It is the flash of a firefly in the night. It is the breath of a buffalo in the wintertime. It is the little shadow which runs across the grass and loses itself in the sunset."
— CROWFOOT, BLACKFOOT (1890, ON HIS DEATHBED)

Proven Ideas

"Wisdom does not belong to one person. We need to act in accord with wisdom, but it does not belong to anyone. It is the illumination of old and proven ideas through generation after generation of discovering natural law."

— Hunbatz Men, Maya, Daykeeper

In the Beginning

"In the beginning we were told that the human beings who walk about on the Earth have been provided with all of the things necessary for life. We were instructed to carry love for one another, and to show a great respect for all the beings of this Earth. We were shown that our well-being depends on the well-being of the vegetable life, and that we are close relatives of the four-legged beings."

— Basic Call to Consciousness: *Haudenosaunee Address to the Western World, Akwesasne Notes*

All Things Are Bound Together

"Humankind has not woven the web of life. We are but one thread within it. Whatever we do to the web, we do to ourselves. All things are bound together. All things connect." — Chief Si'ahl (Seattle), Duwamish-Suquamish

Slow Down

"The elders have been saying for a long, long time, that the world is going to go faster. Things have always happened; there have always been big storms, and earthquakes, floods, and fires, but now they are happening fast, and it's accelerating. It's going to go a lot faster. Because of this, it's real important that we start to slow down."

— David Gehue, Mi'kmaq, at *Cry of the Earth*

Simplicity and Open-Heartedness

"The dark power of the declining Fourth World cannot be destroyed or overpowered. It's too strong and clear for that, and that is the wrong strategy. The dark can only be transformed when confronted with simplicity and open-heartedness. This is what leads to fusion, a key concept for the emerging era."

— Carlos Barrios, Maya-Hispanic

We Never Argue About Creator

"When we discuss or debate things we do it in a respectful manner. That's always been the way here. But while earthly things may be argued about, we never argue about Creator. We respect differences. That is the tradition here on North America, going back many thousands of years."

— Cjegktoonuppa (Slow Turtle - John Peters), Wampanoag, Massapowau, Director of the Massachusetts Commission of Indian Affairs

After All This, The Great Mystery

"After all the great religions have been preached and expounded, or have been revealed by brilliant scholars, or have been written in fine books and embellished in fine language with finer covers, man—all man—is still confronted with The Great Mystery."

— Chief Luther Standing Bear, Oglala Lakota

Paying Attention

"Central to White Buffalo Woman's message, to all native spirituality, is the understanding that the Great Spirit lives in all things, enlivens all forms, and gives energy to all things in all realms of creation, including earthly life.

"Ancient teachings call us to turn primary attention to the Sacred Web of Life, of which we are a part and with which we are so obviously entwined. This quality of attention—paying attention to the whole—is called among my people 'holiness.'"

— Brooke Medicine-Eagle, Crow

MOTHER EARTH

"Some of the medicine seeds I've planted through my life include reminding women that not only our responsibilities but also our joys of life are because we are women on a female planet. Some women think, 'What's that mean, female planet?' But they've been calling her Mother Earth all their lives."

— AMYLEE, SHIELDMAKER, WOMEN'S CIRCLE GUIDE, RAPTOR REHABILITATOR

OUR ELDERS TELL US

"I feel pain and anger that in your rush toward development, the fabric of this globe has been rent, and that what you call the biosphere or ecosphere—but which my people more simply call Mother—has been so neglected and hurt…

"…Our elders tell us we have to do more than save what is left of our traditional homelands. We need to continue to an overall change of mind…so that human-kind can begin to initiate strategies which will preserve and sustain the environment that all cultures and nations share."

— RUBY DUNSTAN, LYTTON INDIAN BAND

THE SEVENTH GENERATION

"In our way of life with every decision we make we always keep in mind the Seventh Generation of children to come…When we walk upon Mother Earth we always plant our feet carefully, because we know that the lives of future generations are looking up at us from beneath the ground. We never forget them."

— OREN LYONS, FAITHKEEPER, ONONDAGA, AT *CRY OF THE EARTH*

SOMETHING WE MUST HAVE

"Love is something you and I must have. We must have it because our spirit feeds upon it, We must have it because without it we become weak and faint. Without love our self-esteem weakens. Without it our courage fails. Without love we can no longer look confidently at the world. We turn inward and begin to feed upon our own personalities and little by little we destroy ourselves. With it we are creative. With it we march tirelessly. With it, and with it alone, we are able to sacrifice for other."

— CHIEF DAN GEORGE, COAST SALISH

ONLY YOU CAN MAKE THIS CRUCIAL CHOICE

"To us, as caretakers of the heart of Mother Earth, falls the responsibility of turning back the powers of destruction. You yourself are the one who must decide. You alone—only you—can make this crucial choice, to walk in honor or to dishonor your relatives. On your decision depends the fate of the entire world. Each of us is put here in this time and this place to personally decide the future of humankind...

"In our prophecies it is told that we are now at the crossroads: Either unite spiritually as a Global Nation, or be faced with chaos, disasters, diseases, and tears from our relatives' eyes...We are the only species that is destroying the Source of Life, meaning Mother Earth, in the name of power, mineral resources, and ownership of land, using chemical and methods of warfare that are doing irreversible damage. Mother Earth is becoming tired and cannot sustain any more impacts of war."

— ARVOL LOOKING HORSE, LAKOTA, AT *CRY OF THE EARTH*

Eagle, Condor, Quetzal

"We are the ones of yesterday. We are the ones of today. We are the ones of tomorrow…Always we have in mind the unification of the Eagle of the North (America) with the Condor of the South (America). When the Eagle flies with the Condor, the Spirit of the land will reawaken. The Eagle and the Condor will be joined together by the Quetzal of the Center (Central America)."

— Don Alejandro Cirilo Perez Oxlaj, Maya

Full Realization

"The eagles of the north cannot be fully realized without the condors of the south, nor can the condors ascend without the eagles…Profound social, political, and spiritual currents are at work in indigenous nations all around the globe. These dynamic currents parallel the obvious dynamic currents in the technology-based cultures. The currents parallel, but do not generally intersect…But they will find each other. In time eagle and condor will fly together in cooperation and peace."

— Iachak Alberto Taxo, Atis (Kichwa), August 9, 1995, on the plaza before UN Headquarters, first International Day of the World's Indigenous Peoples

THE CENTER IS EVERYWHERE

"Peace... comes within the souls of men when they realize their relationship, their oneness, with the universe and all its powers, and when they realize that at the center of the Universe dwells Wakan-Tanka, and that this center is really everywhere, it is within each of us."

— HEHÁKA SÁPA - BLACK ELK, OGLALA LAKOTA

TRY TO UNDERSTAND THINGS

"Spider Grandmother did give two rules. To all men, not just Hopis. If you look at them, they cover everything. She said 'Don't go around hurting each other.' And she said, 'Try to understand things.'"

— KENDRICK FRITZ, HOPI

WE ARE NOT SO DIFFERENT

"Be well, my children, and think good thoughts of peace and togetherness. Peace for all life on earth, and peace with one another in our homes, families, and countries.

"We are not so different in Creator's eyes. The same great Father Sun shines his love on each of us daily, just as Mother Earth prepares the sustenance for our table, do they not? We are one after all."

— DAN EVEHEMA, HOPI

FOUR SACRED TOOLS

"The four sacred tools that native people apply to their lives are honesty, humility, sharing, and respect."

— OJSHIGKWANÀNG (WILLIAM COMMANDA),
TRADITIONAL CHIEF, KITIGAN ZIBI ANISHINABEG

Giving Thanks

"When you arise in the morning
give thanks for the morning light
for your life and strength
give thanks for your food
and the joy of living.

If you see no reason for giving thanks,
the fault lies within yourself."

— Tecumseh, Shawnee

We Do Not Want Riches

"Look at me: I am poor and naked, but I am the chief of the nation. We do not want riches, but we do want to train our children right. Riches would do us no good. We could not take them with us into the other world. We do not want riches. We want peace and love."

— Red Cloud, Lakota

TASTE THE HAPPINESS OF GIVING

"It was our belief that the love of possessions is a weakness to be overcome. Its appeal is to the material part, and if allowed its way it will in time disturb one's spiritual balance. Therefore, children must early learn the beauty of generosity. They are taught to give what they prize most, that they may taste the happiness of giving."

— OHÍYE S'A (CHARLES EASTMAN),
SANTEE DAKOTA, ENGLISH, FRENCH

A WAY TO GIVE BACK

"The most important thing to remember about ceremony is that it is a way for us human beings to give back to Creation some of the energy that we are always receiving. The Earth Mother constantly gives us two-leggeds a surface on which to place our two feet. Father Sun warms us, and Grandmother Moon brings dreams. The element of Earth gives us a place to grow food and the ability to make homes and tools. The water keeps us alive. The fire warms our homes and cooks our food. The air gives us the sacred breath of life…Through ceremony, we learn how to give back."

— SUN BEAR, OJIBWE

CORNERSTONE OF CHARACTER

"Silence is the absolute poise or balance of body, mind, and spirit. The man who preserves his selfhood is ever calm and unshaken by the storms of existence…If you ask him, 'What is silence?' he will answer: 'It is the Great Mystery. The Holy Silence is His voice.' If you ask: 'What are the fruits of silence?' he will say: 'They are self-control, true courage or endurance, patience, dignity and reverence. Silence is the cornerstone of character.'"

— OHÍYE S'A (CHARLES EASTMAN),
SANTEE DAKOTA, ENGLISH, FRENCH

YOU WILL KNOW EACH OTHER

"If you talk to the animals they will talk with you, and you will know each other. If you do not talk to them you will not know them, and what you do not know you will fear. What one fears, one destroys."

— CHIEF DAN GEORGE, COAST SALISH

ESSENCE OF CIVILIZATION

"The man who sat on the ground in his tipi meditating on life and its meaning, accepting the kinship of all creatures and acknowledging unity with the universe of things, was infusing into his being the true essence of civilization. And when native man left off this form of development, his humanization was retarded in growth."

— LUTHER STANDING BEAR, SICANGU AND OGLALA LAKOTA

THE FIVE-FINGERED ONES

"The last 500 years have been about conquest and domination. The next 500 years need to be about healing the damage, and building a better future…Our children are asking for that. All of us have to walk together, side by side, not one in front or behind. It's no longer the red man or the yellow man, or the black man or the white man. It's a journey of all the five-fingered ones."

— NAA T'ÁANII LEON SECATERO, IINA'BI'HO

IT'S NOT A DONE DEAL

"It is the choice of each generation whether or not the prophecies of life's disintegration and dissolution will actually fully manifest in that generation's time. It is not a 'done deal' where fears—as well as desires—of apocalyptic visions are concerned."

— OREN LYONS, FAITHKEEPER, ONANDAGA

UNDER THE SACRED TREE

"He (Crazy Horse) saw his people being driven into spiritual darkness and poverty while others prospered in a material way all around them. But even in the darkest times he saw that the eyes of a few of his people kept the light of dawn and the wisdom of the Earth, which they passed on to some of their grandchildren.

"...he saw a time come when his people began to awaken, not all at once, but a few here and there, and then more and more, and he saw that they were dancing in the beautiful light of the Spirit World under the Sacred Tree even while still on Earth. Then he was amazed to see that dancing under that tree were representatives of all races who had become brothers, and he realized that the world would be made new again and in peace and harmony, not just by his people, by members of all the races of mankind."

— VINSON BROWN, HUMAN BEING, AUTHOR

ALL ARE TOGETHER IN THE SACRED CIRCLE

"Mind of separation, mind of domination—these have birthed genocide of native people throughout the world, the Inquisition, the Nazi holocaust in Europe, the destruction of lands, cultures, and peoples in Asia, and the invention of weaponry with the power to kill all people on Earth twenty times over.

"In the Tsalagi teachings, such great sufferings are seen as unnecessary. They are the result of pride, the idea that one is better or more important than another.

"In reality, in the circle of right relationship, there is no above and no below, no in or out—all are together in the sacred circle."

— VEN. DHYANI YWAHOO, ETOWAH BAND, TSALAGI (CHEROKEE)

Warriors of the Rainbow

"The indigenous tribes were not surprised when the Black, White, and Yellow peoples arrived on their shores, because their prophecies had spoken of the coming of other races. They knew that the new tribes would overwhelm the ancient cultures of the land they called Turtle Island…But it was said that in our times the spirit of the Indian would be born anew into all of the races that have gathered in this land. A portion of the different races of the rainbow colors will see that we are all one family. These Warriors of the Rainbow will bring with them a new time of living in harmony with our environment and with all peoples."

— Heyoka Merrifield, Cherokee-Crow

WHAT DOES IT MATTER?

"The color of the skin makes no difference. What is good and just for one is good and just for the other, and the Great Spirit made all men brothers.

"I have a red skin, but my grandfather was a white man. What does it matter? It is not the color my skin that makes me good or bad."

— WHITE SHIELD, ARIKARA (SOUTHERN CHEYENNE)

FLOWERS IN GREAT SPIRIT'S GARDEN

"We are all flowers in the Great Spirit's garden. We share a common root, and the root is Mother Earth. The garden is beautiful because it has different colors in it, and those colors represent different traditions and cultural backgrounds."

— GRANDFATHER DAVID MONONGYE, HOPI

So It Is In Everything

"You have noticed that everything an Indian does is in a circle, and that is because the Power of the World always works in circles, and everything tries to be round. The sky is round, and I have heard that the earth is round like a ball, and so are all the stars. The wind, in its greatest power, whirls. Birds make their nests in circles, for theirs is the same religion as ours…Even the seasons form a great circle in their changing, and always come back again to where they were. The life of a man is a circle from childhood to childhood, and so it is in everything where power moves."

— Heháka Sápa - Black Elk, Oglala Lakota

Honor and Respect

"To honor and respect means to think of the land and the water and plants and animals who live here as having a right equal to our own to be here.

"We are not the supreme and all-knowing beings, living at the pinnacle of evolution, but in fact we are members of the sacred hoop of life, along with the trees and rocks, the coyotes and the eagles, and fishes and toads, that each fulfills its purpose. They each perform their given task in the sacred hoop, and we have one, too."

— Wolf Song, Abenaki

CARETAKERS

"We must all become caretakers of the Earth."

— HAIDA GWAII, TRADITIONAL CIRCLE OF ELDERS

ALL IS MADE NEW

"When humans participate in ceremony, they enter a sacred space. Everything outside of that space shrivels in importance. Time takes on a different dimension. Emotions flow more freely. The bodies of participants become filled with the energy of life, and this energy reaches out and blesses the creation around them. All is made new; everything becomes sacred."

— SUN BEAR, OJIBWE

SACRED PLACES

"To encounter the sacred is to be alive at the deepest center of human existence. Sacred places are the truest definitions of the earth; they stand for the earth immediately and forever; they are its flags and shields. If you would know the earth for what it really is, learn it through its sacred places."

— N. SCOTT MOMADAY, KIOWA-CHEROKEE

FIND WAYS

"He (Peacemaker) said that as human beings have the capability of thinking, human beings can reach the conclusion that peace is a more appropriate state of being than war. All human beings who are capable of thinking will thus want to find ways to reach peace..."

— JOHN MOHAWK, SENECA, HAUDENOSAUNEE

LOOK AHEAD

"Look behind you. Then see your sons and your daughters. They are your future. Look farther ahead and see your sons' and your daughters' children and their children's children even unto the Seventh Generation. That's the way we were taught. Think about it: you yourself are a Seventh Generation."

— TADODAHO LEON SHENANDOAH, ONONDAGA, HAUDENOSAUNEE, *AT CRY OF THE EARTH*

Original Instructions

"There is a phrase that is used among many of our elders these days: 'Remember the original instructions.' These original instructions are beyond dogma; they are the patterns encoded within the DNA helix at the core of our genetic makeup.

"Just as a guitar being tuned in one part of a room sets the strings of a piano in another part of the room to vibrating, so does the tuning of the universe set our minds in motion…

"Patterns of suffering have been seeded by the dissonance between what is ideal and what is. Movement toward the ideal—including the hopes and prayers of all beings—creates pathways for resolution."

— Ven. Dhyani Ywahoo, Etowah Band, Tsalagi (Cherokee)

Natural Laws

"The original instructions are natural laws that were given to our people by Creator, including the idea of respecting all things as part of the sacred circle of life.

"We are the generation with the responsibility and option to choose the path with a future for our children. We must join hands with the rest of creation, and speak of common sense, responsibility, brotherhood, and peace."

— Oren Lyons, Onondaga Faithkeeper, at Cry of the Earth

Not Ideas, But Reality

"Native people refer to the *original instructions* often in speech and prayer, but rarely attempt to say exactly what they are. They are not like the Ten Commandments carved in stone. They are not ideas. They are reality. They are natural law. They are the way thing are–the operational manual for a working creation—and they cannot be totally understood in words. They must be experienced.

"The original instructions are not imposed by human minds on the world. They are of the living spirit. Other creatures follow them instinctively, and they are communicated to humankind through the heart, through feelings of beauty and love.

"The original instructions urge us to find our place in the cosmos, to know our true nature and our goal in existence. There must be a response—not an intellectual answer—but a felt understanding of the nature of this existence, of its purpose and of our part in that purpose. That is the reason for the spiritual quests, the religions, the rituals, the searches, pilgrimages, meditations, and all the mystic disciplines of humankind. Something in our consciousness is just not satisfied with only eating, sleeping, creating, and reproducing. Something in us wants to know what it's all about and how we fit into it."

— Manitonquat (Medicine Story), Assonet Band Wampanoag

You Are the Foundation of the Thousand Years of Peace

"The prophecies of the Lakota-Dakota have stated that you are the foundation of the thousand years of peace. But first there must be a spiritual purification by fire and water. With that purification comes truth."

— Ta Kola Ota (Darrell Dale Standing Elk), Sicangu Lakota

Great Law of Peace

"The Giver of Life—Creator—did not intend that people abuse one another. Therefore, human societies must form governments that prevent the abuse of human beings by other human beings and ensure peace among nations and peoples.

"Peace is the product of a society that strives to establish reason and righteousness. 'Righteousness' refers to the shared ideology of the people using their purest and most unselfish minds.

"All people have a right to the things they need to survive—even those who do not or cannot work. No people or person has a right to deprive others of these things: food, clothing, shelter, and protection.

"Human beings should use every effort to sit in council about, arbitrate, and negotiate their differences. Force should be resorted to only as a defense against the certain use of force."

— Great Law of Peace, Haudenosaunee

Let Us Put Our Minds Together

"Although different people have different ways of understanding the truth, there is only one Creator. All of us, no matter what our beliefs, come from this Creator. That's why when Indian people gather we always say, 'Let us put our minds together and have one mind.' We know that.

"The Creator created us equal...Sometimes we think we are superior; but no, we are all equal in the eyes of the Creator. If anyone is higher it may be the children, for they are the purest and the closest to the Mystery."

— Ojshigkwanàng (William Commanda),
Traditional Chief, Kitigan Zibi Anishinabeg

Always Ask Permission

"Never take a leaf or move a pebble without asking permission. Always ask permission. That maintains the balance and teaches humility. That leaf you want to pluck could be far more important than the little purpose you have in mind. You don't know. So ask permission first. We can't go on this way with the modern culture. Plants, species, and animals are dying, We need to listen to the spirits and bring them back."

— Don José Matsuwa, Huichol

SEVERAL PROPHECIES

"We have several prophecies concerning the time we are living in, and it is in fulfillment of the Prophecies that we are here today. I will mention some of them: At the time of the 13 Baktun and 13 Ahau is the time of the return of our Ancestors and the return of the men of wisdom. That time is now.

"Another one says: 'Arise, everyone, stand up!' Not one, nor two groups be left behind the rest. This prophecy is in reference to all: rich or poor, black or white, men or women, indigenous or non-indigenous, we all are equal, we all have dignity, we all deserve respect, we all deserve happiness; we all are useful and necessary to the growth of the country and to make a nation where we can live with respect among the different cultures.

"We the Indigenous People join together in defense of the life of the human species, in defense of the life of our brother animals and the trees and in defense of the life of Mother Earth, because the life of the Planet Earth is in danger…

"… In each period of the Sun there is an adjustment for the planet and it brings changes in the weather conditions and in social and political life as well…

"…The world is transformed and we enter a period of understanding and harmonious coexistence where there is social justice and equality for all. It is a new way of life….

"...The Mayan prophecies are announcing a time of change. *The Pop Wuj*, the Book of Counsel, tells us it is time for dawn. Let the dawn come, for the task to be finished."

— DON ALEJANDRO CIRILO PEREZ OXLAJ, MAYA

WHIRLING RAINBOW

"The Whirling Rainbow is the promise of peace among all Nations and all people. The Rainbow Race stresses equality and opposes the idea of a superior race that would control or conquer other races. The Rainbow Race brings peace through the understanding that all races are one. The unity of all colors, all creeds working together for the good of the whole, is the idea that is embodied in the Whirling Rainbow. When all pathways to wholeness are respected by all cultures, the prophecy of the Whirling Rainbow will be completed."

— JAMIE SAMS, SENECA-CHEROKEE-FRENCH

The Next 500 Years

"The journey we are beginning now is for the next 500 years. What will be the sacred path that people will walk over the next 500 years? Even in the midst of all the changes taking place and all the things falling apart, we are building that foundation now. That's something important for us to remember and to focus on. If we don't do it, no one else will.

"All anyone needs to do is look around. We have been destroying nature systematically for many decades. Now nature is destroying us with winds and storms and earthquakes and volcanoes. All that was known a long time ago. The elders have been telling us for years that this would come. Now it's here and it's hurting us.

"...All the native knowings, or prophecies that have been passed down talk about a time when the five-fingered ones (human beings) would be so caught in the illusion of separation that they would forget their original instructions. This forgetting has caused terrible suffering for everyone and everything. It is very important for us to reconnect our life and our ways.

"Things are changing, and in the midst of this the most important thing is the sacred path to the next 500 years, creating that path in a sacred manner with positive thoughts and actions. We have experienced negativity on a mass scale. There is social illness; there is great pain and suffering in our world. Those kinds of negativity and social illnesses we do not need to take along this new pathway into the next 500 years. If we do, we only become sicker.

"What is so very important in our lives now—just like water, we need it all the time—is recognition that there is sacredness in every form. When you put all that together you have a process of what I call 'sacredization,' a fundamental recognition of the sacredness of all things. That, I feel, is a part of our original instructions as human beings.

"...We are all asking ourselves 'what do we do next?' Our ending time has come, and we are now asking for the best possible way to restructure, reset, and put things back on track that give strength to us. So we have a huge task. We are going to have to come together. This pathway into the next 500 years has to be open, so that we can bring in sacredness. We want to make a beginning, a pathway, a Blessingway for this next 500 years. That's the task that is before all of us right now."

— NAA T'ÁANII LEON SECATERO, IINA'BI'HO

FUSION

"The date specified in the Mayan calendar—Winter Solstice in the year 2012—does not mark the end of the world. Many outside people writing about the Mayan calendar sensationalize this date, but they do not know. The ones who know are the indigenous elders who are entrusted with keeping the tradition. Humanity will continue, but in a different way. Material structures will change. From this we will have the opportunity to be more human.

"All the prophecies of the world, all the traditions, are converging now. There is no time for games. The spiritual ideal of this era is action. High magic is at work on both sides, the light and the dark. Things will change, but it is up to the people how difficult or easy it is for the changes to come about.

"...We live in a world of polarity: day and night, man and woman, positive and negative. Light and darkness need each other. They are a balance. Just now the dark side is very strong, and very clear about what they want. They have their vision and their priorities clearly held, and also their hierarchy.

"...On the light side everyone thinks they are the most important, that their own understandings, or their group's understandings, are the key. There's a diversity of cultures and opinions, so there is competition, diffusion, and no single focus...

"The dark side works to block fusion through denial and materialism. It also works to destroy those who are working with the light to get the Earth to a higher level. They like the energy of the old, declining Fourth World, the materialism. They do not want it to change. They do not want fusion. They want to stay at this level, and are afraid of the next level.

"The dark power of the declining Fourth World cannot be destroyed or overpowered. It's too strong and clear for that, and that is the wrong strategy. The dark can only be transformed when confronted with simplicity and open-heartedness. This is what leads to *fusion*, a key concept for the World of the Fifth Sun...

"...The greatest wisdom is in simplicity. Love, respect, tolerance, sharing, gratitude, forgiveness. It's not complex or elaborate. The real knowledge is free. It's encoded in your DNA. All you need is within you. Great teachers have said that from the beginning. Find your heart, and you will find your way."

— CARLOS BARRIOS, MAYA-HISPANIC

WE CANNOT WAIT

"I, myself, have a very quick message from the women of indigenous peoples...We are in very, very difficult times, and it becomes an individual kind of thing for people to change their lifestyle for the things going on upon the earth to change. We cannot wait for large amounts of money from huge committees or organizations to make the changes for us."

— CLAN MOTHER AUDREY SHENANDOAH, ONONDAGA, HAUDENOSAUNEE, AT CRY OF THE EARTH

ONE HEART, ONE MIND

"We must stand together, the four sacred colors of humanity, as the one family that we are, in the interest of peace. We must abolish nuclear and conventional weapons of war. We must raise leaders of peace. We must unite the religions of the world as a spiritual force strong enough to prevail in peace We human beings are a spiritual energy that is thousands of times stronger than nuclear energy. Our energy is the combined will of all people with the spirit of the natural world to be of one body, one heart, and one mind for peace."

— TADADAHO LEON SHENANDOAH, ONONDAGA, HAUDENOSAUNEE, AT CRY OF THE EARTH

FORGIVENESS

"Forgiveness is the way to transmute poison and pain. It can replace negative emotions with positive ones... Forgiveness is not to 'forget'...Forgiveness is personal; the benefits are personal...When we share our stories of humanness, we find healing."

— OJSHIGKWANÀNG (WILLIAM COMMANDA),
TRADITIONAL CHIEF, KITIGAN ZIBI ANISHINABEG

UNIVERSAL CONSCIOUSNESS

"Our vision is for the peoples of all continents, regardless of their beliefs in the Creator, to come together as one at their Sacred Sites to pray and meditate and commune with one another, thus promoting an energy shift to heal our Mother Earth and achieve a universal consciousness toward attaining peace."

— CHIEF ARVOL LOOKING HORSE, LAKOTA, 19TH GENERATION
KEEPER OF THE WHITE BUFFALO CALF PIPE

REMEMBER WHO YOU ARE

"When are you going to be an elder? I showed you; you know what I have. You've been around long enough to be an elder. Quit looking elsewhere. Remember who you are. The origins are within you."

— GRANDFATHER MARTIN M. MARTINEZ, DINÉ

FOUR QUESTIONS

"My grandfather, Sagoyewatha (RedJacket) offered simple teachings. For example, each person should ask himself or herself four important questions that can serve as guides.

"Am I happy in what I am doing? Is what I am doing going to add to the confusion in the world? What am I doing to bring about peace and contentment? And, how will I be remembered when I am gone?"

— YEHWENODE (TWYLAH NITSCH), SENECA

REMEMBER THE KEY

"In these times of turmoil, every human being is being asked to remember their connection to Creator and to the Earth Mother, making those connections strong. Each person's connection to the Great Mystery, to the Earth Mother, to the spirits of the ancestors and to their spiritual essences holds the key to finding the balance…

"…Human beings tend to forget that no man-made organization is The Source. The only Source is Great Mystery, Creator. Every human being must answer to that Source, not to another human being."

— JAMIE SAMS, SENECA-CHEROKEE-FRENCH

SACRED WEB

"The people who are living on this planet need to break with the narrow concept of human liberation, and begin to see liberation as something that needs to be extended to the whole of the natural world. What is needed is the liberation of all things that support life—the air, the waters, the trees—the things which support the sacred web of life."

— BASIC CALL TO CONSCIOUSNESS: HAUDENOSAUNEE ADDRESS TO THE WESTERN WORLD, AKWESASNE NOTES

CONSIDER SERIOUSLY

"We are now living in the fourth and final world of the Hopi. We are at a most critical time in human history. It is a crossroads at which the outcome of our actions will decide the fate of all life on earth.

"...This is the last world. We are not going anywhere from here. If we destroy this, the highest world, which is like heaven, we will be given no other chances...

"...Let us consider this matter seriously so that this world is not destroyed, so that we can continue to live and save this land and life for the generations to come."

— MARTIN GASHWESEOMA, HOPI, AT *CRY OF THE EARTH*

SIMPLE LIFE

"The Great Spirit based us here to take care of this land and life for Him through prayer, meditations, ceremonies, and rituals, and to lead a simple life close to the Earth. That's what we have been doing. Governments talk all the time about human rights, equality, justice, and all those things, but they have never done anything for the native people. Never.

"It's time that they do that—live up to their talk—otherwise nature is going to take over. Earthquakes, flooding, destruction by volcanic eruptions, tidal waves, things like that. It's already happening, and it takes that kind of thing to wake up many people who are controlling this land by money and power and just ripping everything from the Earth. They are doing something that is not right in the law of the Great Spirit and the law of nature. We're all going to have to work together. The world is in trouble right now."

— THOMAS BANYACYA, HOPI, AT *CRY OF THE EARTH*

PATH TO SURVIVAL

"Brothers and sisters: We bring to your thoughts and minds that right-minded human beings seek to promote above all else the life of all things.

"We direct to your minds that peace is not merely the absence of war, but the constant effort to maintain harmonious existence between all peoples, from individual to individual, and between humans and the other beings of this planet.

"We point out to you that a spiritual consciousness is the path to survival of humankind."

— HAUDENOSAUNEE DECLARATION

— IN BEAUTY, TOGETHER MAY WE WALK —

About the Compiler

Independent journalist Steven McFadden is the author of over a dozen nonfiction books, including: *Legend of the Rainbow Warriors; Profiles in Wisdom; Keys for Adept Aging;* and *Classical Considerations: Harvard Master John H. Finley, Jr.*

(Author photo 2008/E. Wolf)

He is co-author *of Farms of Tomorrow* and *Farms of Tomorrow Revisited.* He independently authored *The Call of the Land: An Agrarian Primer for the 21st Century;* also *Awakening Community Intelligence;* and *Deep Agroecology: Farms, Food, and Our Future.*

In 1992-93 he served as National Coordinator for Earth Day USA, and helped develop the Council Circles community protocol in partnership with the Seventh Generation Fund.

Odyssey of the 8th Fire, Steven's epic, nonfiction saga of the Americas is freely available online <8thFire.net>

Sample reviews of
Steven McFadden's books

Library Journal on *Profiles in Wisdom:* "This wise and provocative collection is highly recommended."

New York Times Book Review: "*Profiles in Wisdom* does a fine job not only of presenting the dignity, complexity, and wit of important Indian philosophers and religious leaders, but also of issuing cautions against easy uplift and wisdom injections...There are some stirring and unexpected powers unleashed in this book."

The Washington Times on *Profiles in Wisdom*: "Our leaders should sit and listen to the counsel Steven McFadden has gathered in this book."

Headline Muse: "In the wake of the September 11 tragedies, *The Legend of the Rainbow Warriors* is of added import. Clearly, human existence is experiencing profound shifts of consciousness...As one struggles to make sense of these recent events...McFadden offers substantive insight and hope. Further, he speaks to the power of individuals to address the overwhelming and complex problems facing us today—locally as well as globally."

Odyssey Magazine on *Legend of the Rainbow Warriors*: "I urge everyone on the spiritual path to read this small yet exceptionally powerful book."

Resurgence Magazine on *Farms of Tomorrow*: "It is rare to come across any practical farming guide that sets out, from its inception, a set of principles that embrace social, spiritual and economic concerns on completely equal terms…The wisdom and clarity of philosophy are striking throughout."

Whole Earth Review on *Farms of Tomorrow*: "This is the best book to access the Community Supported Agriculture (CSA) movement, including philosophical, spiritual, practical essays and how-to (including financial discussions). This is the source for tools, organizations, farms, and networks concerning the renewal of agriculture."

Midwest Book Review: "…*Deep Agroecology* is more than the promotion of another growing system. It represents a fundamental change in the perceptions of humans about the choices they make in planting, harvesting, and eating food…The result is a hard hitting, powerful survey that takes the food system ideal a step further…"

Deep Agroecology: Farms, Food, and Our Future

"Thank you, Steven McFadden, for rich and moving clarity, as you weave for us the many threads of '*deep* agroecology.' The vision you capture is not a choice, for in this dire moment for our Earth, it is life's only possibility forward." ~ Frances Moore Lappé, author, *Diet for a Small Planet* and cofounder of Food First and the Small Planet Institute

Soul*Sparks Books

Soul*Sparks Books is an imprint of Light and Sound Press, LLC, an independent venture of married partners Elizabeth Wolf and Steven McFadden.

As an independent enterprise we are self-directed and self-governing. We are free of affiliation with any organization, government, religion, financial institution, or other entity. As publishers we are salutary. By that we mean our intentions and actions are focused on supporting healthy improvement in the natural environment, as well as in the realm of human development.

The word "spark" conveys the idea of something small but active, exciting, and filled with potential and spiritual fire. That's the basic editorial and artistic vision that we hold for the Soul*Sparks series of gift books.

Other Soul*Sparks Books

Keys for Adept Aging

*

A Primer for Pilgrims

*

Tales of the Whirling Rainbow:
Myths & Mysteries for Our Times

*

Classical Considerations:
Musings Prompted by
The Late Harvard Master John H. Finley, Jr.

*

Awakening Community Intelligence:
CSA Farms as Twenty-first Century Cornerstones

Soul*Sparks Books

An imprint of Light and Sound Press, LLC
Tiwa Territory, Albuquerque, New Mexico, U.S.A.

SoulSparksBooks.com

LightAndSoundPress.com